The Best Tagine Recipes

Original Moroccan Tagine Recipes for You and Your Family

It is time for you to travel into the depths of the Moroccan cuisine and discover its hidden secrets and mouth-watering recipes.

Who said you do not get to taste and fall in love with the amazing and famous Moroccan Tagines without visiting Morocco?

Now, you will have it in your home and in your own kitchen.

Table of Contents

Introduction

I want to thank you and congratulate you for purchasing this recipe book.

Moroccan cuisine is a harmonious and memorable combination of oriental colors and Arab hospitality. This is a cuisine, wrapped in the fragrance of spices and mint tea, and generously flavored with the hot sun of the North of Africa.

Tagine can be called a symbol of Moroccan cuisine. Tagine is not just a dish, but also the pottery in which it is cooked. It is unusual and beautiful, and there is, honestly, something fabulous about it. Pay attention to the dome cover. It is not only decorative, but has a meaning. And all this because, due to the domed shape of the cover, a special condensation of steam is obtained. Tagine is cooked for a long time and at low heat. Steam, soaked in the aromas of spices, rises, condenses on the walls of the dome, and flows back into the ingredients. A constant circulation of moisture inside the tagine pottery is obtained. Thanks to this process, the dishes cooked in this special pottery turn out to be extraordinarily tender and juicy.

Moroccan tagine is hot and spicy, sweet, and fragrant, with a thick sauce-like syrup. This dish consists of tender meat, fish, or vegetables stewed to perfection in a thick buttery sauce, with fruits, herbs, spices, and often honey and chili.

Nowadays, we can enjoy tagine, thanks to the Berbers, the indigenous people of northern Africa and Egypt. Although tagine is a Berber dish, other people living at different times in Morocco influenced its taste and preparation. This includes Arabs, the descendants of the Mauritanians, who moved from Andalusia, the Sephardic Jews, and the French colonialists.

How to use tagine?

Traditional clay Moroccan tagine pottery should be soaked overnight. This way, the clay will absorb the moisture, which will be then gradually given up to the dish, and it extends its life, since water will reduce the likelihood of cracking. Clay will gradually absorb spices and flavors over the years, and the dishes cooked in such pottery will be tasty and unusual. Since the Moroccans cook in a tajine pottery on charcoal, this dish should not be used on a gas stove without a special flame divider.

After preparation, the tagine pottery should be washed and dried. It should be covered with the lid only when it is on the dry plate to prevent the creation of mold in the clay.

Modern dishware manufacturers use enameled cast iron when making the lower part of the tagine. This is convenient, as the dish can be lightly fried before extinguishing. And to take care of such pottery easier. It is enough simply to lubricate it periodically with vegetable oil and calcine on a plate.

How to cook in tagine?

Cooking in tagine is simple. It is enough simply to add all the ingredients into a clay plate pottery, with water and cover it with a lid. After a while, it is better to reduce the heat and cook until ready. In the end, add a little oil.

In enameled cast-iron tagine pottery, it is better to fry the vegetables with a little oil first, then add the meat or poultry and cover. Then everything as written above.

Dishes in the tagine cannot be prepared within a few minutes - this is a long process that does not make you stumble to the stove, lifting the lid and stirring without end. Tagine would react negatively to such actions. For a successful result, you need not peek into a vessel too often. There will be irreplaceable loss of aromas, saturating the dish, enveloping and soaking in it for hours.

What to cook in tagine?

Meat in the tagine is prepared long enough, from two hours or more. Chicken, fish and vegetables do not need such a long time. But they also become very delicious in the tagine, as they acquire a special texture and aroma. It retains moisture within itself, hence the juiciness. Heat treatment occurs from below - through the bottom of the tagine, and from above - thanks to steam processing.

Most often, when cooking tagine, first you fry onions in it, adding spices to it, then meat or fish. Vegetables or fruits usually are added near the end of the cooking. Here, everything depends on the recipe. During cooking, you will ask yourself, "Should I add any liquid?" Adapted recipes sometimes include water or broth in the ingredients list. Addition of liquid is not forbidden. But only a tiny bit. The thing is that meat, fish, vegetables give juices. At the end of cooking, you should have a thick syrupy sauce. If you add water, it will be excessively liquid and will dilute the natural aroma of meat and spices. Everything tastes better in its own juice!

Which tagine should I buy?

Moroccans often cook in ordinary clay tagine pottery. There are several types, glazed and painted, which are used for serving on the table.

Pottery is good because it absorbs spices and oils, so with each next time, your tagine will be more and more tasty. When choosing the pottery, make sure it has a thick and heavy bottom. Traditionally, Moroccans prepare their tagine on smoldering coals, since standard clay tagine pottery is not entirely adapted for domestic gas or electric cookers. If you have a gas stove, buy a divider. If you have electric, then choosing a tagine with a thick bottom, and use it carefully. For cooking tagine at home, especially on an electric stove, it is preferable to buy tagine made from heat-resistant ceramics or enameled cast iron of one of the well-known brands. Cast iron is good because meat can be fried on it before cooking. In the north, in Tangier and Casablanca, where the Spanish and French influence on the local cuisine is evident, the meat is pre-fried. In Fez and Marrakech, tagines are often prepared by simply adding all the ingredients and adding a little water and cooking oil in the end.

Tagine pottery can be of different sizes - both portioned and large enough to cook dinner for 12 or more people. I advise you to choose your own according to the size and appetite of your family.

After removing the lid, you can serve your dish on the table right at the bottom. The base is shallow and is made this way for a reason. The Moroccans are serving a ready dish in the pottery or are shifting it into a more beautiful version of the tagine.

If you have not bought specialized pottery yet, try cooking the tagine in a cast iron deep frying pan. I promise, soon you will want to buy the right traditional pottery!

Let's move on to the secrets of cooking.

Chicken and Duck Tagines

Sweet Chicken and Pears Tagine

Serves: 4 to 6

Ingredients:

- 1 whole chicken
- 2 pears, sliced
- 2 onions, sliced
- 30 g of butter
- 7 tablespoons of olive oil
- 1 bunch coriander, chopped
- 3 cinnamon sticks
- ½ cup of water
- 2 tablespoons of honey
- 2 tablespoons of fresh ginger, chopped
- 2 bay leaves
- 1 teaspoon of turmeric
- 1 teaspoon of salt
- 1 teaspoon of ground coriander
- 1 teaspoon sesame seeds
- Black pepper, to taste

Directions:

1. Cut the chicken into pieces then place in a big bowl.
2. In a small bowl, mix the turmeric with the ground coriander, salt, and 5 tablespoons of olive oil, then mix them well and rub the chicken pieces with the marinade.
3. Fry the onion with 2 tablespoons of olive oil in the bottom of the tagine.
4. Place the chicken on top of the onion in the tagine and top it with cinnamon sticks then crush the bay leaves and sprinkle them on top.
5. Add the fresh coriander with water and ginger.
6. Preheat the oven on 350° F and allow the tagine to cook in it for 50 minutes.
7. While the chicken is stewing, you can caramelize the pears. In a preheated frying pan, heat the butter then caramelize it with the sliced pear and honey for almost 5 minutes.
8. Once the chicken is finished stewing, add the pears to the tagine and cook them for another 10 minutes.
9. Pour the sauce of the caramelized pear on top, sprinkle it with sesame seeds, then serve it warm and enjoy.

Couscous and Apricot Tagine

Serves: 4

Ingredients:

- 800 g skinless and boneless chicken, cut into chunks
- 1 ½ cup of of chicken broth
- 50 g dry raisins
- 2 onions, thinly sliced
- 65 g dry apricots
- 2 tablespoons of flour
- 2 tablespoons of lemon juice
- 2 tablespoons of tomato purée
- 1 teaspoon of cinnamon powder
- 1 ½ teaspoons of ground ginger
- 1 ½ teaspoons of ground cumin
- ½ teaspoon of freshly ground black pepper
- ¼ teaspoon of curry powder
- 1 cup of boiling water
- 200 g couscous
- Salt, to taste

Directions:

1. In a tagine, combine the raisins with chicken, apricots, and onion, then set them aside.
2. In a small bowl, mix the rest of the ingredients, except for the boiling water and couscous, then pour it on top of the chicken and the other ingredients. Stew them on low heat for 5 hours.
3. Once the time is up, place the couscous in a bowl then pour the boiling water on top of it and allow it to rest for 5 minutes.
4. Serve the chicken tagine with the couscous and enjoy.

Chicken Tagine with Veggies

Serves: 6

Ingredients:

- 2 chicken breasts, cut into chunks
- 400 g of chickpeas
- 400 g of tomatoes, chopped
- 1 butter squash, chopped
- 1 carrot, chopped
- 1 potato, chopped
- ½ onion, chopped
- 3 garlic cloves, minced
- 1 tablespoon of vegetable oil
- 2 cups of vegetable broth
- 1 tablespoon of lemon juice
- 1 tablespoon of granulated sugar
- 1 teaspoon of ground coriander
- 1 teaspoon of black pepper
- 1 teaspoon of salt

Directions:

1. In a preheated pan, heat the oil then use it to brown the onion with garlic for 5 minutes.
2. Once the time is up, place all the ingredients in a tagine, starting with the onion and garlic, chicken, and veggies, then sprinkle the rest of the ingredients on top. If you have no tagine, you can use a slow cooker.
3. Allow them to cook for almost 1 hour and 15 minutes until the veggies and chicken become tender.
4. Serve it warm with bread and enjoy.

Chicken Tagine with Apricots

Serves: 6

Ingredients:

- 6 chicken thighs
- 1 red onion, cut into half rings
- 500 g of apricot, cut in half, remove bone
- 2 tablespoons of honey
- 1 cup of chicken broth or water
- 1 teaspoon of cinnamon
- 1 teaspoon of ginger
- ¼ teaspoon of black pepper
- ¼ of sesame seeds
- 3-4 sprigs of cilantro
- 40 g of butter
- Cayenne pepper, to taste
- Salt, to taste

Directions:

1. Melt the butter in the base of the tagine pot. Add the spices, stir, and fry the spices in the oil for one minute.
2. Add pieces of chicken, as it should be mixed with butter and spices. Lightly fry them on all sides (3 minutes each).
3. Add onion, mix. Cook for another 5 minutes. Pour in broth (water), add coriander and salt. Cover with a top and put on for 20 minutes.
4. Add apricots, overlaying the chicken. Top with a sprinkle of honey.
5. Close the lid again and leave for 5 minutes. Open the lid, turn over the apricots, and give it another 5 minutes.
6. Serve with couscous, sprinkle with sauce, and decorate with sesame seeds.

Chicken Tagine with Green Beans

Serves: 6

Ingredients:

- 8-10 chicken thighs
- 300 g of green beans
- 2 large onions
- 4 cloves of garlic
- 1 bunch of parsley and cilantro
- 1 preserved lemon
- 2 tablespoons of olive oil
- ½ teaspoon of ginger powder
- 1 teaspoon of turmeric
- Freshly ground black pepper, to taste
- Salt, to taste

Directions:

1. Peel and finely chop onions and garlic. Preheat oil in a tagine and fry onion until transparent, approximately 5 minutes.
2. Add the ginger powder and turmeric, put chicken, and fry until golden brown on all sides. Pour in enough water to

cover the bottom, close the lid, and cook on low heat for 1 hour.

3. Add a bouquet of half the greens and beans, salt, pepper, close, and simmer at minimum heat for about 20 minutes. Remove the bouquet of greens.

4. Slice on thin long straws half of preserved lemon. Chop finely and mash in a mortar in the paste the remaining piece of lemon, then mix it with the remaining finely chopped greens, and add to the tagine.

5. Serve immediately, sprinkle with straws of preserved lemon.

Nutty Chicken Thighs with Apricots

Serves: 4 to 6

Ingredients:

- 900 g of chicken thighs
- 800 g of canned chickpeas, drained
- 2 cups of tomatoes, diced
- 2 cups of water
- 1 cup of dry apricots
- 1 onion, sliced
- 4 tablespoons of olive oil
- 2 tablespoons of garlic, grated
- 2 tablespoons of fresh ginger, grated
- 1 ½ tablespoon of honey
- ½ tablespoon of cumin
- ½ tablespoon of turmeric
- ¼ cup of almonds, sliced
- Black pepper, to taste
- Salt, to taste

Directions:

1. Heat the oil in a tagine and fry the onion with garlic for 4 minutes.
2. Add chicken thighs and cook for 3 minutes.
3. Stir in the rest of the ingredients, except for the tomatoes and almonds, then cook them until they start boiling.
4. Lower the heat and put on the lid then let them cook for 1 hour on low heat.
5. Once the time is up, add the tomatoes then cook the stew for 15 minutes on low heat.
6. Garnish your tagine with the sliced almonds then serve it warm. Enjoy.

Chicken Tagine with Raisins and Onion

Serves: 4

Ingredients:

- 2 chicken breasts
- 100 g of raisins
- 3 medium onions, sliced
- 1 teaspoon of turmeric
- 3 tablespoons of vegetable oil
- ¼ teaspoon of cinnamon
- 2 tablespoons of granulated sugar (optional)
- 1 ½ cup of water
- ¼ teaspoon of black pepper
- Salt, to taste

Directions:

1. In a tagine line up the slices of onion then top it with the chicken. Pour the oil on top and sprinkle with spices.
2. Allow them to cook for 5 minutes then add the water, cover them, and allow them to cook for 15 minutes.

3. When the time is up, add the raisins on the top and sprinkle the sugar, then let cook until the onion and chicken become soft.
4. Serve it warm and enjoy.

Tangy Chicken and Cauliflower Tagine

Serves: 4 to 6

Ingredients:

- 700 g of chicken, cut into pieces
- 400 g of tomatoes, diced
- 2 cups of cauliflower florets
- 1 cup of water
- 1 yellow onion, finely chopped
- ½ cup of olives, pitted and halved
- 2 tablespoons of olive oil
- 2 teaspoons of cumin
- 2 teaspoons of coriander
- ¼ teaspoon of turmeric
- ¼ teaspoon of cinnamon
- Black pepper, to taste
- Salt, to taste

Directions:

1. Heat the oil in a tagine and fry the onion with garlic for 3 minutes.
2. Add the chicken with the spices and cook for another 3 minutes.
3. Add the water then put on the lid and let them cook for 20 minutes over low heat.
4. Once the time is up, add the cauliflower with the olives and cook for 15 minutes over low heat.
5. Add the tomatoes on top then cook for 12 minutes over low heat.
6. Serve it warm and enjoy.

Sweet and Spicy Chicken Stew

Serves: 4 to 6

Ingredients:

- 1 kg of chicken pieces
- 2 cups of canned tomatoes, diced
- 2 cups of water
- 1 cup of mixed dry fruits of choice
- 1 yellow onion, finely chopped
- 3 tablespoons of oil
- 3 tablespoons of honey
- ½ tablespoon of harissa (hot pepper paste)
- ½ teaspoon of cumin
- ½ teaspoon of turmeric
- ½ teaspoon of cinnamon
- Black pepper, to taste
- Salt, to taste

Directions:

1. Place the dry fruits in a small saucepan and cover with boiling water.
2. Bring to a boil then cook until they soften, then drain them.

3. Heat the oil in a tagine, then fry the onion for 4 minutes.
4. Add the chicken and cook for 3 minutes.
5. Stir the rest of the ingredients, including the dry fruits, then bring to a boil.
6. Lower the heat and put on the lid then cook for 40 minutes.
7. Serve it warm and enjoy.

Chicken and Butternut Squash Tagine

Serves: 4

Ingredients:

- 4 chicken pieces
- 1 cup of small onions, peeled
- 1 cup of butternut squash, cut into chunks
- 1 tablespoon of honey
- 2 teaspoons of coriander seeds, chopped
- ¼ teaspoon of ginger powder
- 2 garlic cloves, chopped
- 2 tablespoons of vegetable oil
- 2 cinnamon sticks
- 1 pinch saffron threads
- 1 pinch cayenne pepper
- Black pepper, to taste
- Salt, to taste

Directions:

1. Spread the chicken pieces with salt and pepper. Then, heat the oil in a tagine and brown the chicken in it.
2. Take the chicken pieces and set them aside. Then, brown the onion with garlic in the tagine for 1 minute.
3. Once the time is up, add the chicken pieces and stir the rest of the ingredients and bring them to a simmer. Lower the heat and cook it for 20 minutes covered.
4. Serve your tagine warm with bread and enjoy.

Chicken Stew Tagine

Serves: 4 to 6

Ingredients:

- 1 ½ kg of chicken thighs, skinless
- 2 cups of water
- 1 sweet potato, diced
- ½ butternut squash, peeled and diced
- 3 tablespoons of vegetable oil
- 2 tablespoons of lemon juice
- 1 teaspoon of cinnamon
- 1 teaspoon of ginger
- 1 teaspoon of turmeric
- 2 cloves of garlic, minced
- Black pepper, to taste
- Salt, to taste

Directions:

1. Heat the oil in a tagine then brown chicken thighs for 3 minutes on each side.
2. Add the rest of the ingredients.
3. Put on the lid and cook for 1 hour on low heat.
4. Once the time is up, serve your tagine warm. Enjoy.

Artichoke Hearts and Chicken Tagine

Serves: 4 to 6

Ingredients:

- 1 kg of chicken, cut into pieces
- ½ kg of artichoke hearts
- 2 ½ cup of water
- 1 cup of olives
- 1 cup of green peas
- 1 yellow onion, finely chopped
- 1 bunch of fresh coriander, finely chopped
- 1 preserved lemon
- 3 tablespoons of olive oil
- 1 teaspoon of turmeric
- 1 teaspoon of cumin
- 1 teaspoon of ground ginger
- Black pepper, to taste
- Salt, to taste

Directions:

1. Heat the oil in a tagine and fry the onion for 3 minutes.
2. Add the chicken pieces and cook for 6 minutes.
3. Add the spices, water, coriander, and artichoke hearts, then put on the lid and cook for 25 minutes over low heat.
4. Add the preserved lemon with olives and peas.
5. Put on the lid and cook for 15 to 20 minutes or until the chicken is done.
6. Once the time is up, serve your tagine warm and enjoy.

Chicken and Chickpeas Tagine

Serves: 4 to 6

Ingredients:

- 8 chicken thighs
- ½ teaspoon of ginger powder
- ½ cup of green olives
- 1 onion, finely chopped
- 2 teaspoons of turmeric powder
- 1 teaspoon of cinnamon
- 1 teaspoon of cumin
- ½ cup of chicken broth
- 4 to 6 cups of couscous, cooked
- Black pepper, to taste
- Salt, to taste

Directions:

1. Combine all the ingredients, except for the couscous, in the tagine or the slow cooker. Then, reduce the heat to low and allow it to cook for 3 to 4 hours in a slow cooker or 1 hour in a tagine.
2. Once the time is up, serve it with couscous and enjoy.

Classic Chicken and Potato Tagine

Serves: 4 to 6

Ingredients:

- 700 g of chicken, cut into pieces
- 4 potatoes, peeled and quartered
- 2 cups of water
- ½ cup of green olives
- ¼ cup of parsley, finely chopped
- 1 preserved lemon
- 2 tablespoons of vegetable oil
- ½ teaspoon of turmeric
- ½ teaspoon of cumin
- ¼ teaspoon of ginger
- 2 cloves of garlic, minced
- Black pepper, to taste
- Salt, to taste

Directions:

1. Heat the oil in a tagine and fry garlic with chicken for 4 minutes.
2. Add the water with spices, parsley, a pinch of black pepper,

and a small pinch of salt.
3. Put on the lid and cook for 20 minutes over low heat.
4. Add the potato quarters on top, then put on the lid and cook for 10 minutes.
5. Top them with the preserved lemon and olives, then put on the lid and let them cook for an extra 10 minutes.
6. Serve your tagine warm and enjoy.

Ancient Chicken Fennel Tagine

Serves: 4 to 6

Ingredients:

- 1 kg of chicken, cut into pieces
- 2 fennel bulbs, quartered
- 1 cup of chickpeas, soaked and drained
- 1 yellow onion, finely chopped
- 3 tablespoons of vegetable oil
- 3 tablespoons of parsley, finely chopped
- 2 teaspoons of cumin
- 1 teaspoon of ginger
- Black pepper, to taste
- Salt, to taste

Directions:

1. Heat the oil in tagine and fry the onion for 3 minutes.
2. Add the rest of the ingredients, then put on the lid and cook for 45 minutes to 1 hour over low heat.
3. Once the time is up, serve your tagine warm and enjoy.

Green Olives Chicken and Chermoula Tagine

Serves: 4 to 6

Ingredients:

- 1 kg of chicken, cut into dices
- 200 g of chicken liver
- 2 onions, finely chopped
- 2 cups of water
- 1 cup of green olives, pitted and halved
- 1 small preserved lemon, cut into strips
- 4 tablespoons of parsley, finely chopped
- 3 tablespoons of vegetable oil
- 1 teaspoon of turmeric
- 1 teaspoon of cumin
- 1 teaspoon of ginger
- 2 cloves of garlic, minced
- Black pepper, to taste
- Salt, to taste

Directions:

1. Bring a small saucepan of water to a boil then cook the chicken liver until it done.
2. Drain the chicken livers and cut them into small dices.
3. Combine the garlic with parsley and half the preserved lemon in a small mortar then crush them until they become like a paste.
4. Toss the mix with the chicken in small mixing bowl and place it aside.
5. Heat the oil in a tagine then fry the onion for 5 minutes.
6. Add the chicken mix with spices then cook for 4 minutes.
7. Once the time is up, stir in the chicken livers with water, a pinch of salt and pepper.
8. Put on the lid and let them cook for 30 minutes over low heat.
9. Once the time is up, add the olives with the rest of the preserved lemon and cook for an extra 20 minutes.
10. Serve your tagine warm and enjoy.

Tagine Roasted Chicken with Raisins

Serves: 4

Ingredients:

- 850 g of chicken, cut into pieces
- 2 cups of water
- 1 large white onion, thinly sliced
- ¼ cup of raisins
- 3 tablespoons of vegetable oil
- 1 tablespoon of granulated sugar
- 1 teaspoon of turmeric
- 1 teaspoon of ginger
- ½ teaspoon of cinnamon
- Black pepper, to taste
- Salt, to taste

Directions:

1. Heat the oil in a tagine then brown the chicken on all sides.
2. Add the spices with water and onion then put on the lid and cook for 45 minutes over low heat.
3. Sprinkle the raisins on top then put on the lid and cook for an extra 15 minutes.
4. Serve your roasted chicken raisins warm and enjoy.

Chicken and Rice Tagine to Die For

Serves: 4

Ingredients:

- 850 g of chicken, cut into pieces
- 5 cups of water
- 1 ½ cup of rice, uncooked
- 1 small onion, finely chopped
- ¼ cup of green olives
- 3 tablespoons of vegetable oil
- 2 tablespoons of coriander, finely chopped
- 1 teaspoon of turmeric
- ½ teaspoon of ginger
- ½ teaspoon of cumin
- Black pepper, to taste
- Salt, to taste

Directions:

1. Heat the oil in a tagine then brown the chicken pieces on both pieces.
2. Pour the rice all over it, followed by the spices, coriander and water.
3. Put on the lid and cook for 45 minutes over low heat.

4. Add the green olives on top then put on the lid and cook for an extra 15 minutes over low heat.
5. Serve your chicken and rice tagine warm and enjoy.

Fennel and Peas Tagine

Serves: 6

Ingredients:

- 1 kg of chicken, cut into pieces
- 1 onion, chopped
- 200 g of fennel
- 200 g of peas, fresh or frozen
- 3 tablespoons of vegetable oil
- 1 teaspoon of turmeric
- 1 tomato, chopped
- 2 cups of water
- ¼ teaspoon of black pepper
- Salt, to taste

Directions:

1. Fry the chicken with onion and oil in a tagine or pot, then add the peas and fennel, followed by the spices and water.
2. Allow it to cook until all ingredients become soft, then remove the cover, add the tomato, and allow it to simmer for 15 minutes.
3. Serve it warm and enjoy.

43

Mushrooms Chicken Tagine

Serves: 4 to 6

Ingredients:

- 1 kg of chicken, cut into pieces
- 400 g of mushrooms, sliced
- 2 cups of water
- 1 yellow onion, thinly sliced
- ½ cup of green olives
- 2 tablespoons of olive oil
- 1 teaspoon of turmeric
- 1 teaspoon of ginger
- ¼ teaspoon of cumin
- Black pepper, to taste
- Salt, to taste

Directions:

1. Heat the oil in a tagine and fry the onion for 3 minutes.
2. Add the chicken and cook for other 4 minutes.
3. Stir in the rest of the ingredients then put on the lid and cook for 45 minutes over low heat.
4. Serve your mushrooms tagine warm and enjoy.

Pears Steak Tagine

Serves: 4 to 6

Ingredients:

- 2 kg of chuck steak, cut into pieces
- 2 fresh pears, seeded and quartered
- 2 yellow onions, finely chopped
- 2 cups of water
- ½ cup of honey
- The juice of 1 lemon
- 3 tablespoons of vegetable oil
- 2 tablespoons of Moroccan spice blend
- 1 tablespoon of butter
- 1 teaspoon of allspice, ground
- 1 teaspoon of cinnamon
- ½ teaspoon of turmeric
- Black pepper, to taste
- Salt, to taste

Directions:

1. Heat half the oil in a tagine and brown the steak pieces for 4 minutes then drain it and place it aside.
2. Add the rest of the oil to the tagine and heat it.
3. Fry the onion with garlic for 4 minutes.
4. Add the Moroccan spice blend with the browned steak pieces, ginger, a pinch of salt and pepper.
5. Add the water then put on the lid and let cook for 2 hours over low heat.
6. Meanwhile, bring a medium saucepan of water to a boil.
7. Place in it the pear slices and cook for 5 minutes until they soften.
8. Melt the butter in a large frying pan and fry the pear slices for 3 to 5 minutes on each slice until they become golden brown.
9. Add the honey and stir them until the pears caramelize.
10. Place the pear slices on top of the steak tagine and drizzle the remaining honey in the pan all over it.
11. Put on the lid and let the tagine cook for 8 minutes.
12. Serve it warm with sesame seeds and enjoy.

Sunny Olives and Chicken Meatballs Tagine

Serves: 4 to 6

Ingredients:

- 700 g of lean chicken, minced
- 2 tomatoes, finely chopped
- 1 yellow onion, finely chopped
- 4 to 6 eggs, to your liking
- ½ cup of water
- ¼ cup of green olives, pitted and sliced
- 3 tablespoons of coriander, finely chopped
- 3 tablespoons of vegetable oil
- 1 teaspoon of paprika
- 1 teaspoon of turmeric
- 1 teaspoon of cumin
- ½ teaspoon of chili paste
- ¼ teaspoon of ginger
- Black pepper, to taste
- Salt, to taste

Directions:

1. Combine the lean chicken meat with ½ teaspoon of paprika, ½ teaspoon of turmeric, and ½ teaspoon of cumin, ginger, 1 tablespoon of coriander, a pinch of salt and pepper then knead with your hands to combine the flavors.
2. Shape the mix into small bite size meatballs and place them on a lined baking sheet.
3. Heat the oil in a tagine then fry the onion for 3 minutes.
4. Add the rest of the spices with tomatoes, water, and coriander then put on the lid and cook for 10 minutes over low heat.
5. Drop in the chicken meatballs then scatter the slices olives on top.
6. Put on the lid and cook for 12 minutes over low heat.
7. Once the time is up, crack eggs on top then put on the lid and cook for other 10 minutes or until the eggs are done to your liking.
8. Serve your tagine warm and enjoy.

Eggplant Chicken Tagine

Serves: 4 to 6

Ingredients:

- 1 kg of chicken, cut into pieces
- 200 g of green beans, trimmed
- 200 g of carrot, cut into strips
- 2 eggplants, diced
- 1 small white onion, thinly chopped
- 4 cups of water
- 1 cup of tomato purée
- 3 tablespoons of olive oil
- 2 tablespoons of parsley, finely chopped
- 2 teaspoons of turmeric
- 2 teaspoons of ginger
- ¼ teaspoon of black pepper
- Salt, to taste

Directions:

1. Heat the oil in a tagine then fry the onion for 4 minutes.
2. Add the chicken with ginger, turmeric, parsley, black pepper and salt then cook for 3 minutes.

3. Add the water, tomato purée, veggies and then put on the lid and cook for 40 minutes over low heat.
4. Serve your eggplant chicken tagine with couscous and enjoy.

Roasted Chicken and Mushrooms Tagine

Serves: 4 to 6

Ingredients:

- 1 kg of chicken thighs
- 400 g of mushrooms
- 3 cups of water
- 1 yellow onion, finely chopped
- 4 tablespoons of parsley, finely chopped
- 4 tablespoons of vegetable oil
- 1 preserved lemon, minced
- 1 teaspoon of cumin
- 1 teaspoon of turmeric
- Black pepper, to taste
- Salt, to taste

Directions:

1. Combine the parsley with preserved lemon and crush until they become like a paste.
2. Toss the chicken in a mixing bowl with the parsley and lemon mix, spices, a pinch of salt and pepper.
3. Heat the oil in a tagine then brown the chicken thighs for 3 to

5 minutes on each side.

4. Remove the chicken and place it aside.
5. Add the onion to the tagine and cook it for 4 minutes.
6. Add back the chicken with mushrooms and water then put on the lid and cook for 45 minutes over low heat.
7. Serve your tagine warm with Moroccan bread and enjoy.

Original Chicken and Fries Tagine

Serves: 4 to 6

Ingredients:

- 1 kg of chicken, cut into pieces
- 3 cups of water
- 1 preserved lemon
- 4 tablespoons of vegetable oil
- 2 tablespoons of coriander, finely chopped
- 2 tablespoons of parsley, finely chopped
- 4 cloves of garlic, peeled
- 1 teaspoon of turmeric
- 1 teaspoon of ginger
- Black pepper, to taste
- Salt, to taste

Directions:

1. Combine the preserved lemon with garlic, coriander and parsley in a mortar and crush, until they become like a paste.
2. Place the chicken in a tagine then pour the garlic mix all over it, followed by the spices and water.
3. Put on the lid and cook for 45 minutes.
4. Serve chicken tagine with French fries and enjoy.

Carrot and Peas Chicken Tagine

Serves: 4 to 6

Ingredients:

- 1 kg of chicken, cut into pieces
- 4 cups of water
- 2 cups of snow peas
- 1 cup of carrot, diced
- 1 cup of tomatoes, grated
- ¼ cup of parsley, finely chopped
- 3 tablespoons of vegetable oil
- 2 tablespoons of fresh lemon juice
- 1 teaspoon of turmeric
- 1 teaspoon of ginger
- 1 teaspoon of cumin
- Black pepper, to taste
- Salt, to taste

Directions:

1. Heat the oil in a tagine then brown the chicken pieces for 2 min on each side.
2. Scatter over it the peas and carrot dices.
3. Mix the spices with coriander, tomatoes and water in a mixing bowl then pour it all over the chicken and veggies.
4. Put on the lid and cook for 45 minutes over low heat until the chicken is done.
5. Serve your chicken tagine warm and enjoy.

Sweet Almond Chicken Couscous Tagine

Serves: 4 to 6

Ingredients:

- 1 whole chicken
- 250 g of prunes
- 5 cups of water
- 4 tablespoons of almonds, peeled and fried
- 4 tablespoons of raisins
- 1 small yellow onion, finely chopped
- 4 tablespoons of vegetable oil
- 1 teaspoon of turmeric
- 1 teaspoon of ginger
- ½ teaspoon of cinnamon
- Black pepper, to taste
- Salt, to taste

Directions:

1. Heat the oil in a tagine then brown the whole chicken on all sides.
2. Add onion and cook for 2 minutes.

3. Stir in the water with spices then put on the lid and cook for 45 minutes over low heat.
4. Meanwhile, bring a small salted pot of water to a boil and cook the prunes until they become soft.
5. Drain the prunes and add them to the tagine with almonds and raisins.
6. Drizzle the honey on top then put on the lid and cook for 15 minutes.
7. Serve your tagine with couscous and enjoy.

Chicken Liver Tagine

Serves: 4 to 6

Ingredients:

- 750 g of chicken liver, diced
- 2 cups of water
- 1 large yellow onion, finely chopped
- 4 tablespoons of parsley, finely chopped
- 3 tablespoons of vegetable oil
- 3 cloves of garlic, minced
- 1 teaspoon of paprika
- 1 teaspoon of turmeric
- ¼ teaspoon of ginger
- Black pepper, to taste
- Salt, to taste

Directions:

1. Bring a saucepan of water then cook in it the chicken livers for 10 minutes.
2. Heat the oil in a tagine and fry the onion for 3 minutes over low heat.
3. Add the spices with parsley and garlic then cook for 1 minute.

4. Add the livers with water and put on the lid then let cook for 12 minutes over low heat.
5. Serve your chicken liver tagine warm with rice and enjoy.

Roasted Turkey with Chickpeas and Olives

Serves: 4 to 6

Ingredients:

- ♦ 1 kg of turkey pieces
- ♦ 3 cups of water
- ♦ 1 large yellow onion, thinly sliced
- ♦ 1 cup of canned chickpeas, drained
- ♦ 1 cup of green olives
- ♦ 1 preserved lemon
- ♦ 1 bunch of fresh coriander, finely chopped
- ♦ 3 tablespoons of olive oil
- ♦ 3 cloves of garlic, minced
- ♦ 1 teaspoon of cumin
- ♦ 1 teaspoon of turmeric
- ♦ ½ teaspoon of ground ginger
- ♦ Black pepper, to taste
- ♦ Salt, to taste

Directions:

1. Heat the oil in a tagine or stew pot then brown the turkey pieces until they become golden brown.
2. Remove the turkey pieces and place them aside.
3. Add the onion with garlic to the tagine and cook for 4 minutes.
4. Add the cumin with ginger and turmeric then cook for 1 minute.
5. Add the water with coriander, turkey, a pinch of salt and pepper then bring to a boil.
6. Put on the lid and lower the heat then cook the stew for 30 minutes.
7. Add the olives with chickpeas and preserved lemon then put on the lid and cook for an extra 15 minutes over low heat.
8. Once the time is up, adjust the seasoning of the turkey tagine then serve it warm and enjoy.

Lamb and Goat Tagines

Spicy Goat Meat

Serves: 4 to 6

Ingredients:

- 1 kg of goat meat
- 2 cups of chicken broth
- 4 tomatoes, chopped
- 3 green cardamom pods
- 1 onion, sliced
- 1 onion, chopped
- 3 bay leaves
- 1 cinnamon stick
- 1 teaspoon of salt
- ½ teaspoon of cayenne pepper
- ½ teaspoon of turmeric
- 1 pinch saffron
- ½ teaspoon of black pepper
- 3 garlic cloves, chopped
- 1 tablespoon of honey
- 3 tablespoons of vegetable oil
- ½ teaspoon of cumin

Directions:

1. Heat 2 tablespoons of oil in a tagine, fry garlic and the chopped onion for 3 minutes, then add all the spices, except for the honey, and allow them to simmer in the oil for 30 seconds.
2. Add the goat meat to the tagine and fry for 1 minute, coating it with the aromatic spices mix for 1 minute.
3. Add the cardamom, cinnamon, bay leaves, and chicken broth, bring it to a boil then allow it to simmer for 2 hours on low heat.
4. In another pot, warm the remaining tablespoon of oil and fry the onion for 4 minutes, then add a pinch of salt and the chopped tomatoes, while stirring every once and a while for 40 to 45 minutes on low heat.
5. Add the honey and allow them to cook for other 2 minutes.
6. Once the goat meat has become well-cooked and you can easily take it off the bone, remove it from the tagine and allow the broth to simmer for at least other 15 minutes or more, then serve it with onion and tomatos. Enjoy.

Tomato and Goat Tagine

Serves: 4

Ingredients:

- 1 kg of goat stew meat
- 2 cups of chicken broth
- 1 onion, diced
- 2 tablespoons of ghee
- 4 cups of tomatoes, finely chopped
- 1 cinnamon stick
- 2 tablespoons of dry apricots
- 1 teaspoon of paprika
- 1 teaspoon of ginger
- 1 teaspoon of cumin
- ½ teaspoon of turmeric
- 1 teaspoon of dry coriander, grinded
- Black pepper, to taste
- Salt, to taste

Directions:

1. Fry the onion with ghee in a tagine for 3 minutes. Add the goat meat and cook for 7 minutes.
2. Add the rest of the ingredients and cover the tagine. Cook it for 2 hours on low heat.
3. Serve your tagine warm and enjoy.

Tomato and Lamb Tagine

Serves: 4

Ingredients:

- 500 g of lamb meat
- 3 large tomatoes, sliced into rings
- 2 medium onions, sliced into rings
- 2 cups of water
- 1 tablespoon of honey
- ½ teaspoon of turmeric
- ½ teaspoon of black pepper
- ½ teaspoon of ground ginger
- 3 tablespoons of vegetable oil
- ½ teaspoon of cinnamon powder
- Salt, to taste

Directions:

1. Place the oil, turmeric, black pepper, 2 cups of water, salt, ginger, and meat into a tagine and bring them to a boil. Reduce the heat to low and place the onion rings on top and allow it to cook until the meat becomes easy to separate from the bones, at least 40 minutes.

2. Add the tomatoes on top of the onion rings and allow it to cook thoroughly for about 20 minutes.
3. When the tomato is well-cooked, remove the tagine from the heat and sprinkle the cinnamon powder on top, followed by the honey.
4. Preheat the oven to 180° F then place the tagine in it, without the cover, and allow it to cook until it becomes caramelized.
5. Serve it warm and enjoy.

Lamb Tomato Sauce Tagine

Serves: 4

Ingredients:

- 500 g of lamb (flesh or ribs)
- 400 g of tomatoes, pureed
- ½ cup of dried apricots
- 2 small onions, finely chopped
- 1 tablespoon of honey
- 3-4 tablespoons of olive oil
- 1 teaspoon of cumin
- ½ teaspoon of cinnamon
- ½ teaspoon of ginger powder
- ½ teaspoon of turmeric
- Black pepper, to taste
- Salt, to taste

Directions:

1. Heat the olive oil in a tagine and fry onions until for 3 minutes.
2. Add lamb and fry for 5 minutes.
3. Add spices. Cook a few more minutes, stirring constantly, so the meat is properly covered with spices.

4. Add dried apricots, honey, and tomatoes.
5. Stir and cover the tagine. Cook it for an hour and a half on low heat.
6. Serve and enjoy.

Tart Apple Lamb Tagine

Serves: 4 to 6

Ingredients:

- 1 kg of lamb
- 4 apples, quartered
- 2 cups of beef broth
- 1 white onion, finely chopped
- ¼ cup of honey
- 3 tablespoons of vegetable oil
- 2 teaspoons of cinnamon
- 1 teaspoon of turmeric
- 1 teaspoon of ginger
- Black pepper, to taste
- Salt, to taste

Directions:

1. Heat the oil in a tagine then fry the onion for 3 minutes.
2. Add the spices and cook for 1 minute.
3. Add the lamb meat and beef broth then put on the lid and cook for 1 hour 30 minutes.
4. Bring a medium saucepan of water to a boil.

5. Add the apples and cook for 10 minutes until they become soft.
6. Heat the honey in another saucepan then stir into it the apple quarters until they are coated.
7. Add the apples on top of the lamb tagine and drizzle the remaining honey on top. Put on the lid and cook for 20 minutes.
8. Serve your apple tagine warm and enjoy.

Juicy Figs and Lamb Tagine

Serves: 4 to 6

Ingredients:

- 1 kg of lamb, cut into pieces
- 250 g of soft figs
- 2 cups of water
- 1 small onion, finely chopped
- 1 cinnamon stick
- 3 tablespoons of oil
- 2 tablespoons of honey
- 2 teaspoons of cumin
- 1 teaspoon of cinnamon
- 1 teaspoon of turmeric
- 1 teaspoon of fresh ginger, peeled and grated
- Black pepper, to taste
- Salt, to taste

Directions:

1. Heat the oil in a tagine and fry the onion for 5 minutes.
2. Add the spices with lamb pieces then cook for 3 minutes.
3. Add the water with cinnamon stick then put on the lid and cook for 1 hour 30 minutes.
4. Meanwhile, bring a medium saucepan of water to a boil then cook the figs 8 minutes.
5. Drain the figs and add them to the tagine then drizzle the honey all over them.
6. Put on the lid and cook for 20 minutes over low heat.
7. Garnish your tagine with some sliced almonds then serve it and enjoy.

Savory Lamb and Olives Stew

Serves: 6

Ingredients:

- 1 ½ kg of lamb
- 2 ½ cups of chicken broth
- 2 yellow onions, diced
- 1 preserved lemon, sliced
- ½ cup of kalamata olives
- 5 tablespoons of vegetable oil
- 1 tablespoon of cumin
- ½ tablespoon of turmeric
- Black pepper, to taste
- Salt, to taste

Directions:

1. Heat the oil in a tagine and fry the onion for 6 minutes.
2. Add the lamb meat with turmeric, cumin, salt, and pepper then cook for 3 minutes.
3. Add the chicken broth then bring to a boil.

4. Put on the lid and lower the heat then cook for 1 hour.
5. Add the olives with preserved lemons then put on the lid and cook for 15 minutes on low heat.
6. Serve it warm and enjoy.

Spicy Lamb and Chickpeas Tagine

Serves: 6

Ingredients:

- 1 ¼ kg of lamb meat
- 2 cups of tomatoes, canned and diced
- 2 cups of water
- 2 cups of chickpeas, canned and drained
- 1 yellow onion, finely chopped
- 4 tablespoons of vegetable or olive oil
- 3 cloves of garlic, minced
- 1 teaspoon of ginger, ground
- 1 teaspoon of turmeric
- 1 teaspoon of cumin
- ¼ cup of fresh coriander
- Black pepper, to taste
- Salt, to taste

Directions:

1. Heat the oil in a tagine and fry the onion with garlic for 4 minutes.
2. Add the lamb meat and cook for 5 minutes.

3. Add the rest of the ingredients, except for the tomatoes and coriander, then put on the lid and cook for 1 hour 35 minutes.
4. Add the coriander with tomatoes then put on the lid back and cook for 15 minutes on low heat.
5. Serve it warm and enjoy.

Spicy and Sweet Lamb Tagine

Serves: 6

Ingredients:

- 6 lamb shanks
- 4 cups of tomatoes, diced
- 450 g of butternut squash, diced
- 250 g of sweet potatoes, diced
- 450 g of golden potatoes, diced
- 3 cups of yellow onion, diced
- 2 cups of low sodium chicken broth
- 3 garlic cloves, sliced
- 1 tablespoon of fresh ginger, peeled and chopped
- ½ teaspoon of chilli powder
- ½ teaspoon of cardamom
- ½ teaspoon of cumin
- 3 tablespoons of olive oil
- Black pepper, to taste
- Salt, to taste

Directions:

1. Fry the onion with olive oil in a tagine for 5 to 7 minutes.
2. Add the lamb shanks and cook them for other 5 minutes.
3. Add the rest of the ingredients into the tagine and cover it. Cook it on low heat for 3 hours.
4. Serve it warm and enjoy.

Saucy Lamb Meatballs Tagine

Serves: 4 to 6

Ingredients:

- 700 g of lamb meat, minced
- 1 large yellow onion, halved and thinly sliced
- 2 cups of tomatoes, puréed
- 1 cup of water
- 4 tablespoons of coriander, finely chopped
- 3 tablespoons of vegetable oil
- 2 teaspoons of cumin
- 2 teaspoons of ginger
- 2 teaspoons of paprika
- ¼ teaspoon of cinnamon
- 3 cloves of garlic, minced
- Black pepper, to taste
- Salt, to taste

Directions:

1. Combine the lamb meat with garlic, 2 tablespoons of coriander, 1 teaspoon of cumin, 1 teaspoon of ginger, 1 teaspoon of paprika, cinnamon, a pinch of salt and pepper in

a large mixing bowl then knead with your hands to combine the flavors.

2. Shape the mix into bite size pieces and place them on a lined baking sheet.
3. Heat the oil in a tagine then fry the onion for 4 minutes.
4. Add the tomatoes with the rest of the spices, coriander, and water.
5. Put on the lid and cook for 10 minutes over low heat.
6. Add the meatballs and put on the lid then cook for 15 minutes over low heat.
7. Serve your lamb meatballs tagine warm and enjoy.

Peachy Quince and Lamb Tagine

Serves: 4 to 6

Ingredients:

- ♦ 1 kg of lamb meat, cut into pieces
- ♦ 8 quinces, seeded and quartered
- ♦ 3 cups of water
- ♦ 1 large tomato, finely chopped
- ♦ 1 small yellow onion, finely chopped
- ♦ 5 tablespoons of granulated sugar
- ♦ 3 tablespoons of fresh coriander
- ♦ 3 tablespoons of vegetable oil
- ♦ 1 cinnamon stick
- ♦ 1 teaspoon of turmeric
- ♦ 1 teaspoon of ginger
- ♦ ¼ teaspoon of cinnamon power
- ♦ ¼ teaspoon of black pepper
- ♦ Salt, to taste

Directions:

1. Bring a pot of water to a boil then cook the quinces for 15 minutes then drain them.
2. Heat the oil in a tagine and fry the onion for 3 minutes.
3. Add the lamb meat with spices, cinnamon stick, coriander, and water then put on the lid and cook for 30 minutes.
4. Add the cooked quinces then put on the lid back and cook for 30 minutes over low heat.
5. Add the chopped tomato all over them with the granulated sugar and put on the lid. Let the tagine cook for an extra 20 minutes or until the tomato is cooked.
6. Serve it warm and enjoy.

Artichokes and Peas Tagine

Serves: 4

Ingredients:

- 1 kg of lamb meat
- 200 g of artichokes
- 1 cup of peas, frozen or fresh
- 2 ½ cups of water
- 2 garlic cloves, chopped
- 3 tablespoons of vegetable oil
- 1 tablespoon of parsley, chopped
- 1 teaspoon of turmeric
- ½ teaspoon of ginger
- 1 preserved lemon, sliced
- Black pepper, to taste
- Salt, to taste

Directions:

1. Fry the meat with the oil in a tagine on both sides for 5 minutes, then add the peas and artichokes.
2. Sprinkle a pinch of salt, black pepper, turmeric, ginger, and parsley on top.

3. Add the water and cover the tagine. Cook on low heat until the peas, meat, and artichokes have that buttery texture.
4. Garnish tagine with preserved lemon and enjoy.

Kebab Tagine (Kabab Mardor)

Serves: 2 to 4

Ingredients:

- 250 g of lamb meat, diced
- 3 eggs
- 1 onion, diced
- 1 tablespoon of mix of parsley and coriander
- 2 tablespoons of olive oil
- ½ teaspoon of turmeric
- ¼ teaspoon of black pepper
- ½ cup of water
- Salt, to taste

Directions:

1. Combine all ingredients in a tagine, except the eggs. Cook on low heat for 30 to 40 minutes untill the meat is cooked and become soft.
2. Once the meat is perfectly cooked, whisk the eggs in a bowl then pour it on top of the meat, cover it and cook for other 5 minutes.
3. Serve tagine with Moroccan bread and enjoy.

Lamb with White Bean Tagine

Serves: 4 to 6

Ingredients:

- 200 g of lamb meat, cut into small pieces
- 700 g of white beans, soaked for an overnight
- 1 ½ cup of tomatoes, grated
- 1 small carrot, diced
- 1 teaspoon of turmeric
- 1 teaspoon of ginger
- ¼ teaspoon of cumin
- ¼ teaspoon of paprika
- 1 bay leaf
- Water
- Black pepper, to taste
- Salt, to taste

Directions:

1. Place the white beans in a large pot and cover it with water then put on the lid and cook until it becomes dent.
2. Drain the white beans and place in a tagine.
3. Add the rest of the ingredients, except the tomatoes, then cover with water.

4. Put on the lid and cook for 1 hour over low heat.
5. Add the tomatoes and cook for 10 minutes over low heat.
6. Serve lamb bean tagine warm and enjoy.

Berber Spring Tagine

Serves: 4 to 6

Ingredients:

- 800 g of lamb, cut into pieces
- 250 g of potatoes, cut quartered
- 250 g of carrots, cut into strips
- 4 cups of water
- 1 cup of snow peas
- 1 small onion, finely chopped
- 3 tablespoons of coriander, finely chopped
- 3 tablespoons of vegetable oil
- 1 teaspoon of turmeric
- 1 teaspoon of ginger
- ¼ teaspoon of paprika
- Black pepper, to taste
- Salt, to taste

Directions:

1. Heat the oil in a tagine then fry the onion for 3 minutes.
2. Stir in the lamb with spices, potatoes, carrots, coriander and water then put on the lid and cook for 45 minutes.

3. Add the snow peas then put on the lid and cook for an extra 20 minutes over low heat.
4. Serve your tagine warm with Moroccan bread and enjoy.

Pineapple Tagine

Serves: 4 to 6

Ingredients:

- 1 kg of lamb
- 2 onions, chopped
- 3 tablespoons of vegetable oil
- 50 g of dry prunes
- 250 g of canned pineapple
- 50 g of dry apricots
- ½ teaspoon of saffron
- ½ teaspoon of black pepper
- 2 garlic cloves, chopped
- 1 teaspoon of cinnamon powder
- 3 ½ tablespoons of granulated sugar
- 1 ½ tablespoons of butter
- 2 cups of water
- Salt, to taste

Directions:

1. In a tagine fry the onion with oil for 3 minutes then add the meat and allow it to cook for other 2 minutes.
2. Add the ½ teaspoon of cinnamon, garlic, saffron, a pinch of salt and black pepper, and 1 cup of water, then cover it and allow to cook for 1 hour on low heat, adding water if needed.
3. In the meantime, boil the prunes and apricots and set them aside, then drain the pineapple and set it aside.
4. Place the prunes and apricots in a pan, then add 1 cup of water, 1 tablespoon of sugar, ¼ tablespoon of butter, and ½ teaspoon of cinnamon; allow them to caramelize for 20 to 30 minutes on low heat.
5. Heat a pan and add the pineapple with 2 tablespoons of sugar and caramelize it until you are satisfied.
6. Once everything is done, place the pineapple on top of the meat, followed by the prunes and apricots, then pour in the rest of the caramelized broth.
7. Serve it warm and enjoy.

Iconic Marrakesh Tangia Tagine

Serves: 4 to 6

Ingredients:

- 1 kg of lamb meat, cut into pieces
- 3 cups of water
- 3 tablespoons of olive oil
- 1 tablespoon of smen (salted butter)
- 1 preserved lemon
- 1 ½ teaspoon of cumin
- ½ teaspoon of saffron threads
- Black pepper, to taste
- Salt, to taste

Directions:

1. Stir the saffron threads with water in a small bowl.
2. Place the lamb pieces in a tagine then pour the olive oil on them, followed by the spices, smen, preserved lemon and saffron water.
3. Put on the lid and cook for 1 hour 15 minutes over low heat.
4. Serve your tangia warm with bread and enjoy.

Beef Tagines

Meatballs Tagine with Tomato Sauce

Serves: 4 to 6

Ingredients:

- 1 kg of beef, minced
- 4 tomatoes, peeled
- 1 small onion, chopped
- 1 teaspoon of ginger powder
- 2 teaspoon of sweet pepper powder
- 1 teaspoon of black pepper
- 1 teaspoon of chopped coriander
- 1 garlic clove, chopped
- ½ teaspoon of cinnamon
- Salt, to taste

Directions:

1. In a big bowl, mix the minced beef with ginger, cinnamon, coriander, garlic, and a pinch of salt, half teaspoon of black pepper, and 1 teaspoon of sweet pepper powder. Shape the beef into small to medium meatballs and set them aside.
2. Process the peeled tomatoes in a food processor with some water, then pour in a tagine, pan, or a pot, then add the chopped onion with a half teaspoon of black pepper, a pinch of salt, and 1 teaspoon of sweet pepper powder, then bring to a boil.
3. Lower the heat and allow the tomatoes to cook for 15 minutes with the cover on. Add the beef balls, and allow it to cook on low heat for 10 to 15 minutes (add water if needed).
4. Garnish it with coriander, then serve it warm and enjoy.

Beef Tagine with Dry Prunes

Serves: 4 to 6

Ingredients:

- 1 kg of beef
- 250 g of dry prunes
- 100 g of almonds
- 3 tablespoons of vegetable oil
- 2 garlic cloves, chopped
- 2 medium onions, chopped
- 1 tablespoon of sesame seeds
- A pinch of saffron
- 1 teaspoon of ginger powder
- 1 teaspoon of cinnamon powder
- ½ teaspoon of black pepper
- 2 tablespoons of granulated sugar
- 2 ½ cups of water
- Salt, to taste

Directions:

1. Fry the onion and meat with oil in a tagine for 5 minutes, then add a pinch of saffron and salt, garlic, black pepper, and ginger.
2. Pour the water from the side of the tagine; try not to pour it on top of the meat. Then allow it to cook on low heat until the meat is fully cooked and buttery.
3. In the meantime, boil the prunes for 15 minutes then remove it from the water and set it aside.
4. In a medium sauce pan, combine the prunes with the sugar, cinnamon, then add half of the broth from the meat, once it is cooked.
5. Bring the broth and prunes to a boil and allow it to cook for other 5 to 10 minutes on low heat.
6. Place the prunes on top of the meat and in the sides of the serving dish or tagine, then pour the rest of the caramelized broth of the prunes on top and garnish it with the almonds and sesame seeds.
7. Serve it warm and enjoy.

Orange and Beef Tagine

Serves: 4 to 6

Ingredients:

- 1 kg of beef, cut into pieces
- 2 cups of water
- 1 cup of dry apricots
- 1 fresh orange, peeled and finely chopped
- 1 yellow onion, finely chopped
- 1 bunch of fresh coriander, finely chopped
- 3 tablespoons of vegetable oil
- 3 tablespoons of honey
- 2 tablespoons of sesame seeds
- 2 cloves of garlic, minced
- ½ teaspoon of turmeric
- ½ teaspoon of ground ginger
- ¼ teaspoon of cinnamon
- ¼ teaspoon of ground allspice
- Black pepper, to taste
- Salt, to taste

Directions:

1. Heat the oil in a tagine and fry the onion for 3 minutes.
2. Add the beef with spices, coriander, and water then cook until they start boiling. Put on the lid and cook for 40 minutes over low heat.
3. Place the dry apricots in a small saucepan and cover with hot water then cook over medium heat until they become soft.
4. Stir the apricots with honey into the tagine then put on the lid and cook for 15 minutes on low heat.
5. Once the time is up, sprinkle the sesame seeds on top then serve your tagine warm and enjoy.

Beef and Carrot Tagine Stew

Serves: 4

Ingredients:

- 1 kg of beef meat stew
- 2 cups of water
- 4 carrots, sliced
- 1 yellow onion, thinly sliced
- ¼ cup of raisins
- 3 tablespoons of olive oil
- 2 tablespoons of honey
- 2 cloves of garlic, minced
- 1 teaspoon of ginger, ground
- ½ teaspoon of turmeric
- ¼ teaspoon of cumin
- ¼ teaspoon of cinnamon
- Black pepper, to taste
- Salt, to taste

Directions:

1. Heat the oil in a tagine and fry the onion for 4 minutes.
2. Stir in the rest of the ingredients then put on the lid and cook for 1 hour 45 minutes on low heat, while adding more broth if needed.
3. Adjust the seasoning of the stew then serve it warm and enjoy.

Sweet Potato and Beef Tagine

Serves: 4 to 6

Ingredients:

- 900 g of beef, cut into pieces
- 500 g of sweet potatoes, diced
- 3 cups of water
- 1 cup of chickpeas
- 1 cup of tomatoes, finely chopped
- 1 yellow onion, finely chopped
- 3 tablespoons of olive oil
- 1 teaspoon of cumin
- 1 teaspoon of turmeric
- ½ teaspoon of ground allspice
- Black pepper, to taste
- Salt, to taste

Directions:

1. Heat the oil in a tagine and fry the onion for 3 minutes.
2. Stir in the rest of the ingredients, except for the veggies, then cook until they start boiling.

3. Lower the heat and put on the lid then cook for 45 minutes over low heat.
4. Add the sweet potatoes, chickpeas and tomatoes then cook for 25 to 30 minutes or until they are done.
5. Serve it warm and enjoy.

Ancient Green Beans and Beef Tagine

Serves: 4 to 6

Ingredients:

- 1 kg of beef meat, cut into chunks
- 700 g of green beans, trimmed
- 4 cups of water
- 2 cups of tomatoes, finely chopped
- 3 tablespoons of vegetable oil
- 3 cloves of garlic, minced
- 1 teaspoon of turmeric
- 1 teaspoon of paprika
- ¼ teaspoon of ginger
- Black pepper, to taste
- Salt, to taste

Directions:

1. Bring a pot of water to a boil and cook the green beans for 10 minutes then drain it and place it aside.
2. Heat the oil in a tagine then fry the garlic with beef meat and spices for 2 minutes.
3. Stir in the water with coriander and put on the lid then cook for 45 minutes over low heat.

4. Add the cooked green beans and cook for 10 minutes.
5. Add the chopped tomatoes and put on the lid again then cook for 18 minutes over low heat.
6. Serve your beef tagine warm and enjoy.

Tropical Mango Tagine

Serves: 4 to 6

Ingredients:

- ♦ 1 kg of beef stew meat
- ♦ 1 yellow onion, thinly sliced
- ♦ 2 cups of fresh mango, diced
- ♦ 2 cups of water
- ♦ 3 tablespoons of vegetable oil
- ♦ 3 tablespoons of honey
- ♦ 1 tablespoon of fresh parsley, finely chopped
- ♦ 1 tablespoon of fresh coriander, finely chopped
- ♦ 1 teaspoon of cinnamon
- ♦ 1 teaspoon of cumin
- ♦ 1 teaspoon of turmeric
- ♦ 1 teaspoon of ginger
- ♦ Black pepper, to taste
- ♦ Salt, to taste

Directions:

1. Heat the oil in a large tagine then fry the onion for 3 minutes.
2. Add the beef with spices, coriander, parsley and oil then cook for another 3 minutes.
3. Add the water then put on the lid and cook for 1 hour over low heat
4. Scatter the mango chunks on top and drizzle the honey on it then put on the lid and cook for an extra 20 minutes.
5. Serve your tagine with rice and enjoy.

Okra Tagine

Serves: 4

Ingredients:

- 200 g of beef
- 500 g of clean okra
- 1 small onion, chopped
- 1 tomato, chopped
- 1 teaspoon of turmeric
- 3 tablespoons of vegetable oil
- ¼ teaspoon of ginger powder
- 2 cups of water
- ¼ teaspoon of black pepper
- Salt, to taste

Directions:

1. Fry the onion and beef with oil in tagine for 5 minutes.
2. Add 2 cups of water, black pepper, salt, ginger, and turmeric, and allow it to cook on low heat for at least 1 hour until the meat become soft.
3. Add the okra to the tagine, then cover it and allow to cook for other 15 minutes on low heat, without stirring it.

4. Pour the tomato on top and cover the tagine again, without stirring the contents. Allow it to cook for 10 minutes.
5. Serve it warm and enjoy.

Sweet Beef and Pear Tagine

Serves: 6

Ingredients:

- 2 kg of beef chuck steak, cut into chunks
- 2 yellow onions, finely chopped
- 2 pears, quartered
- ¾ cup of honey
- 4 tablespoons of Moroccan spice blend
- 2 tablespoons of lemon juice
- 2 tablespoons of vegetable oil
- 2 garlic cloves, finely chopped
- 2 inches fresh ginger, peeled and grated
- 1 teaspoon of cinnamon
- 1 teaspoon of allspice
- 1 ½ cups of cold water
- Black pepper, to taste
- Salt, to taste

Directions:

1. Cook the pears for 25 minutes with the cover on or until the pears soften.
2. Combine the rest of the ingredients in a tagine or a pot with the liquid from cooking the pears.
3. Cover the tagine and then lower the heat and allow it to cook for 1 hour 30 minutes to 2 hours or until the meat is done.
4. Once the time is up, top the meat with pears and raisins. Enjoy!

Dates and Beef Tagine

Serves: 4 to 6

Ingredients:

- 1 kg of beef stew meat
- 400 g of dates, pitted
- 1 white onion, finely chopped
- 1 ½ cup of water
- ¼ cup of honey
- 3 tablespoons of vegetable oil
- 1 teaspoon of cinnamon
- 1 teaspoon of turmeric
- ½ teaspoon of ginger
- ½ tablespoon of sesame seeds
- Toasted almonds, chopped
- Black pepper, to taste
- Salt, to taste

Directions:

1. Heat the oil in a tagine then fry the onion for 3 minutes.
2. Add the spices with beef and water then put on the lid and cook for 1 hour on low heat.
3. Bring a medium saucepan of water to a boil then cook the dates until they become soft for 10 minutes.
4. Drain the dates and scatter them over the meat then drizzle the honey all over them.
5. Put on the lid and cook for 30 minutes over low heat.
6. Once the time is up, garnish your dates and beef tagine with almonds or sesame seeds and enjoy.

Sweet Apples and Raisins Tagine

Serves: 4 to 6

Ingredients:

- 1 kg of beef stew meat
- 1 onion, sliced
- 3 cups of beef broth
- ½ cup of butter
- ½ cup of raisins
- 3 apples, cut into thick slices
- 2 tablespoons of cilantro, finely chopped
- 1 tablespoon of sesame seeds
- 3 tablespoons of vegetable oil
- 1 teaspoon of Moroccan spice blend
- 1 teaspoon of cinnamon
- ¼ teaspoon of saffron
- 2 tablespoons of honey
- Black pepper, to taste
- Salt, to taste

Directions:

1. Heat 1 tablespoon of oil with half of the butter in a tagine. Brown the meat in batches. Stir in the onion and cook them for 3 minutes.
2. In the meantime, fry and melt the butter with 1 tablespoon of honey and a pinch of cinnamon in a skillet. Then, fry the slices of apples, 5 to 7 minutes on each side on low heat.
3. Stir the rest of the ingredients in a tagine and cover it. Then, lower the heat and cook for 2 hours.
4. Serve your beef with apple and sesame seeds.

Berber Merguaz and Potato Tagine

Serves: 4 to 6

Ingredients:

- 700 g of potatoes, thinly sliced
- 500 g of sausages, sliced
- 2 tomatoes, diced
- 1 ½ cup of water
- 1 yellow onion, diced
- 3 tablespoons of vegetable oil
- 1 teaspoon of paprika
- 1 teaspoon of turmeric
- 1 teaspoon of cumin
- Black pepper, to taste
- Salt, to taste

Directions:

1. Heat the oil in a tagine then fry the onion for 4 minutes.
2. Lay on it half the tomatoes, followed by the sliced potatoes, then pour the rest of the tomatoes on top.
3. Sprinkle the spices on top, followed by the water and sausage slices, then put on the lid and cook for 25 minutes over low heat.
4. Once the time is up, serve your sausages tagine hot and enjoy.

Fish and Seafood Tagines

Classic Potato Fish Tagine

Serves: 4 to 6

Ingredients:

- 450 g of golden potatoes, sliced
- 450 g of cod fillets
- 1 preserved lemon, sliced
- 1 ½ cup of water
- 1 onion, sliced
- 3 tablespoons of vegetable oil
- ½ teaspoon of saffron threads
- 3 garlic cloves, sliced
- ½ teaspoon of ginger
- ½ teaspoon of cumin
- ½ teaspoon of paprika
- ½ cup of Kalamata black olives
- Black pepper, to taste
- Salt, to taste

Directions:

1. Combine the cumin with paprika, a pinch of salt, pepper, saffron, and garlic in a small bowl with 4 tablespoons of water and whisk them gently.
2. Lay the onion in the bottom of a tagine. Then, top it with the fish, potatoes, and lemon.
3. Pour the spice mix on the tagine ingredients with water and cook it for 1 hour on low heat.
4. Serve your tagine warm and enjoy.

Salmon Tagine

Serves: 4

Ingredients:

- 500 g of salmon, divided into 4 slices
- 3 green sweet peppers, cut into strips
- 250 g of mushrooms
- 3 carrots, cut into strips
- ½ teaspoon of salt
- ½ teaspoon of sweet pepper powder
- 1 cup of water
- 2 tablespoons of vegetable oil
- 1 teaspoon of cumin
- 3 garlic cloves, chopped

Directions:

1. Line up the pepper strips in a tagine, followed by carrots and the mushrooms and set them aside.
2. In a small bowl, mix the rest of the ingredients, except for the oil and salmon, then set them aside.
3. Pour the oil on top of the salmon and veggies then pour the sauce on top of everything.

4. Cook on low heat until the carrots become soft, 30 minutes, then place the salmon on top and allow it to cook for another 20 to 30 minutes.
5. Garnish it with parsley and enjoy.

Fish and Olives Tagine

Serves: 4 to 6

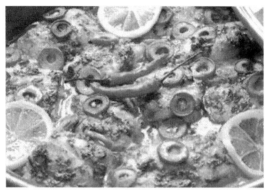

Ingredients:

- 1 kg of white fish fillets
- 1 cup of green olives, sliced
- 2 tomatoes, sliced
- ½ cup of water
- 5 garlic cloves, finely chopped
- ¼ cup of cilantro, finely chopped
- 3 tablespoons of vegetable oil
- 1 tablespoon of lemon juice
- 1 teaspoon of cumin
- Black pepper, to taste
- Salt, to taste

Directions:

1. Place the slices of tomatoes in a tagine and set it aside.
2. Combine the lemon juice with cumin, garlic, cilantro, a pinch of salt, and ginger in a medium bowl to make the marinade. Then, coat the fish with it.
3. Place the marinated fillets on the tomatoes and top it with the

rest of the marinade with oil and olives.

4. Cook the tagine for 25 to 30 minutes on low heat until the fish becomes tender.

5. Serve it warm and enjoy.

Sardines and Potatoes Tagine

Serves: 4 to 6

Ingredients:

- 1 kg of sardines, bones removed
- 2 big potatoes, cut into circles
- 2 tomatoes, cut into circles
- 1 green sweet pepper, roasted and cut into strips
- 1 red sweet pepper, roasted and cut into strips
- 1 cup of water
- 4 garlic cloves, chopped
- 2 tablespoons of mix of coriander and parsley, chopped
- 1 teaspoon of turmeric
- ¼ teaspoon of black pepper
- 1 teaspoon of ginger powder
- ½ teaspoon of chili pepper paste
- 1 teaspoon of sweet pepper powder
- 1 teaspoon of cumin
- ¼ cup of green olives
- Salt, to taste

Directions:

1. In a tagine, place the pepper strips on the bottom, then top it with a layer of tomatoes and potatoes, then set it aside.
2. In a small bowl, combine the parsley and coriander mix with a pinch of salt and the chili paste, ginger, black pepper, cumin, and garlic, then mix them with a half cup of water.
3. Line up the sardines on top of the potatoes with their skin on top, then pour the sauce on top and wash the bowl with the remaining half cup of water then pour it on top of the sardines.
4. Cover the tagine and allow it to cook on low heat until the potatoes become well-cooked, adding water if needed.
5. Garnish tagine with green olives and preserved lemon, then serve it warm and enjoy.

Hot Monkfish Tagine

Serves: 4 to 6

Ingredients:

- 700 g of monkfish fillets, cut into pieces
- 250 g of tomatoes, sliced
- 1 cup of tomatoes, grated
- 1 cup of water
- 2 green bell peppers, sliced
- ¼ cup of parsley, finely chopped
- ¼ cup of black olives
- 2 tablespoons of olive oil
- 1 tablespoon of harissa
- ½ teaspoon of paprika
- ½ teaspoon of turmeric
- 2 cloves of garlic, minced
- 1 bay leaf
- 2 cloves of garlic, minced
- Black pepper, to taste
- Salt, to taste

Directions:

1. Whisk the water with turmeric, parsley, paprika, and harissa in a small bowl.
2. Heat the oil in a tagine then cook the grated tomatoes with garlic for 8 minutes over low heat.
3. Add the monkfish pieces with half the water mix, a pinch of salt and pepper then put on the lid and let cook for 5 minutes.
4. Line up the tomatoes and green pepper slices on top, while alternating between them, then pour the rest of the water mix all over them with a pinch of salt and pepper.
5. Scatter the olives on top then put on the lid and cook for 15 minutes over low heat.
6. Serve your monkfish tagine warm and enjoy.

Marrakech Sardines Tagine

Serves: 4 to 6

Ingredients:

- 1 kg of sardines
- 2 potatoes, peeled and sliced
- 1 large carrot, sliced
- 1 red bell pepper, sliced
- 1 orange bell pepper, sliced
- 2 cups of water
- 1 lemon, sliced
- ½ cup of parsley, finely chopped
- ½ preserved lemon, minced
- 4 tablespoons of vegetable oil
- 1 tablespoon of paprika
- 2 teaspoons of turmeric
- 2 teaspoons of cumin
- 3 cloves of garlic, minced
- Black pepper, to taste
- Salt, to taste

Directions:

1. Mix the garlic with turmeric, cumin, paprika, parsley and preserved lemon, ½ cup of water, a pinch of salt and pepper in a small bowl to make the marinade.
2. Lay the lemon slices, followed by the carrot slices, in the bottom of a tagine then top it with the bell pepper and potatoes.
3. Coat the sardines with the marinade then place them on top and pour the marinade all over them, followed by the oil.
4. Pour the water on the side of the tagine then put on the lid and cook for 25 to 30 minutes over low heat or until the veggies are soft.
5. Serve your tagine warm and enjoy.

Sardines Bites Tagine

Serves: 4 to 6

Ingredients:

- 1 kg of sardines, minced
- 3 cups of white rice, cooked
- 3 large tomatoes, finely chopped
- 1 yellow onion, finely chopped
- ½ cup of water
- ½ cup of coriander, finely chopped
- 4 tablespoons of vegetable oil
- 1 tablespoon of tomato paste
- 2 teaspoons of paprika
- 2 teaspoons of turmeric
- 2 teaspoons of cumin
- 1 teaspoon of paprika
- Black pepper, to taste
- Salt, to taste

Directions:

1. Combine the minced sardines with rice, 1 teaspoon of paprika, 1 teaspoon of cumin, and 1 teaspoon of turmeric, half of the coriander, a pinch of salt and pepper.
2. Mix them with your hands to combine the flavors then shape the mix into bite-size meatballs.
3. Heat the oil in a tagine then fry the onion for 4 minutes.
4. Add the tomatoes with 1 teaspoon of cumin, 1 teaspoon of paprika, 1 teaspoon of turmeric, a pinch of salt and pepper then cook for 5 minutes over low heat.
5. Add the water and put on the lid then cook for an extra 5 minutes.
6. Add the sardines and rice meatballs to the tagine then put on the lid and cook for 20 minutes over low heat.
7. Serve them warm and enjoy.

Juicy White Fish and Cherry Tomato Tagine

Serves: 4 to 6

Ingredients:

- 1 kg of white fish fillets
- 2 potatoes, sliced
- 1 cup of cherry tomatoes, halved
- 1 cup of tomatoes, grated
- 1 cup of water
- 3 tablespoons of parsley, finely chopped
- 1 teaspoon of turmeric
- 1 teaspoon of cumin
- 1 teaspoon of paprika
- ¼ teaspoon of cinnamon
- Black pepper, to taste
- Salt, to taste

Directions:

1. Stir the spices with grated tomatoes, water, a pinch of salt and pepper in a tagine.
2. Cook them until they start boiling.
3. Add the fish fillets with cherry tomatoes and potatoes then put on the lid and cook for 25 minutes or until the potatoes becomes soft.
4. Serve your fish tagine warm and enjoy.

Saucy White Fish Tagine

Serves: 4 to 6

Ingredients:

- 700 g of white fish fillets
- 1 green bell pepper, seeded and sliced
- 1 yellow onion, halved and sliced
- 1 cup of tomatoes, grated
- 1 cup of water
- ¼ cup of green olives, pitted
- ¼ cup of parsley, finely chopped
- ½ green chili pepper, seeded and minced
- 2 tablespoons of olive oil
- ½ teaspoon of turmeric
- ½ teaspoon of cumin
- ½ teaspoon of paprika
- 1 clove of garlic
- Black pepper, to taste
- Salt, to taste

Directions:

1. Whisk the water with turmeric, cumin, tomatoes, parsley, chili pepper, a pinch of salt and pepper.
2. Pour the mix into a tagine and cook until it starts boiling.
3. Lay on it the onion slices, followed by the bell pepper slices, fish fillets and olives.
4. Drizzle the oil all over them then put on the lid and cook for 20 minutes over low medium heat.
5. Serve warm and enjoy.

Spicy Prawns Tagine

Serves: 2 to 3

Ingredients:

- 2 cups of prawns
- 1 small onion, sliced
- 1 canned cup of cherry tomatoes
- ½ cup of chickpeas
- 1 tablespoon of olive oil
- 2 garlic cloves, crushed
- 1 teaspoon of cumin
- 1 tablespoon of harissa paste
- Salt, to taste

Directions:

1. Fry the onion with oil in a tagine for 3 minutes. Then, stir in the garlic with harissa and cumin.
2. Cook them for a 1 minute, and then add the tomatoes and bring it to a simmer for 5 minutes.
3. Stir in the rest of the ingredients and simmer for 5 to 7 minutes.
4. Serve your prawns tagine with some couscous, scattered with mint and coriander and enjoy.

Zesty Hot Seafood Tagine

Serves: 4 to 6

Ingredients:

- 1 kg of white fish, diced
- 250 g of prawns, peeled and deveined
- 150 g of squid, sliced
- 2 cups of tomatoes, grated
- 1 cup of water
- ¼ cup of coriander, finely chopped
- 3 cloves of garlic, minced
- 3 tablespoons of olive oil
- 3 tablespoons of fresh lemon juice
- 2 teaspoons of cumin
- 1 teaspoon of paprika
- 1 teaspoon of cumin
- Black pepper, to taste
- Salt, to taste

Directions:

1. Heat the oil in a tagine then fry the garlic with spices for 1 minute.
2. Add the water with tomatoes then cook until they start boiling.
3. Stir in the rest of the ingredients then put on the lid and cook for 12 minutes over low heat.
4. Serve it warm and enjoy.

Shrimp Tagine with Fennel

Serves: 4

Ingredients:

- 20 large shrimp without head (raw)
- 2 onions, cut into half rings
- 400 g of tomatoes, canned
- 2 fennel bulbs, cut along
- 5 tablespoons of olive oil
- 2 cloves garlic, finely chopped
- 25 g of fresh ginger, grated
- Pinch of saffron
- 1-2 tablespoons of paprika
- A small bundle of cilantro and parsley, finely chop the leaves
- 1 teaspoon of sugar
- Pepper, to taste
- Salt, to taste

Directions:

1. Preheat 3 tablespoons of oil in the tagine, add shrimp, and fry for 2-3 minutes. Add onion, garlic, ginger, and saffron. Cook for 3-4 minutes.

2. Add paprika, tomatoes, and half of the greens. Stir in sugar, add salt and pepper. Put on low heat for 10 minutes. The sauce should thicken.
3. At this time, boil the fennel for 5 to 8 minutes. Then fry it on the remaining oil on both sides until golden brown. Sprinkle with salt and pepper.
4. Stir the shrimp into the sauce, top the fennel, cover the tagine with a lid, and cook for 5 minutes.
5. Serve it warm and enjoy.

Fresh Prawns Tagine

Serves: 4

Ingredients:

- 700 g of prawns
- 8 baby potatoes, quartered
- 2 ½ cups of water
- ½ cup of snow peas
- 1 yellow onion, diced
- ¼ cup of fresh coriander
- ½ preserved lemon, sliced
- 3 tablespoons of olive oil
- ½ teaspoon of cumin
- ½ teaspoon of turmeric
- 3 cloves of garlic, grated
- Black pepper, to taste
- Salt, to taste

Directions:

1. Heat the oil in a tagine and fry onion for 4 minutes.
2. Add the spices and preserved lemon and coriander then cook for 2 minutes.

3. Stir in the water with potatoes and peas then bring to a boil.
4. Put on the lid and cook for 35 minutes on low heat.
5. Stir in the prawns then put on the lid and cook for 6 minutes.
6. Adjust the seasoning of the prawn tagine then serve it and enjoy.

Saucy Squid Tagine

Serves: 4 to 6

Ingredients:

- 750 g of squid, sliced
- 400 g of tomatoes, grated
- 1 cup of water
- ¼ cup of coriander, finely chopped
- 4 tablespoons of vegetable oil
- 2 teaspoons of harissa
- 2 teaspoons of paprika
- 2 teaspoons of cumin
- 1 teaspoon of turmeric
- 2 cloves of garlic, minced
- 1 bay leaf
- Black pepper, to taste
- Salt, to taste

Directions:

1. Heat the oil in a tagine then stir in the spices with grated tomatoes, water, coriander, and garlic.
2. Cook until they start boiling.
3. Stir in the rest of the ingredients then put on the lid and cook for 30 minutes over low heat.
4. Serve your tagine warm and enjoy.

Vegetable Tagines

Dates and Apricots Tagine

Serves: 6

Ingredients:

- 1 ½ cups of veggies broth
- ¼ cup of dates, pitted and halved
- ¼ cup of dry apricots
- 1 brown onion, finely chopped
- 2 carrots, finely chopped
- 1 cup of green beans, trimmed and halved
- 650 g of butternut squash, quartered
- 1 cap of chickpeas
- 2 garlic cloves, crushed
- 2 teaspoons of olive oil
- 2 teaspoons of paprika
- 1 teaspoon of coriander, finely chopped
- 2 saffron threads
- 1 cinnamon stick
- 2 teaspoons of lemon zest
- ½ teaspoon of ginger powder

- ◆ Black pepper, to taste
- ◆ Salt, to taste

Directions:

1. Fry the onions for 5 minutes in a tagine until it softens. Then, stir in the carrot with ginger, cumin, garlic, coriander, paprika, and saffron threads.
2. Cook them for 1 minute then stir in the broth and bring it to a boil.
3. Add the butternut squash to the tagine with beans and apricots. Then, simmer on low heat for 15 minutes.
4. Stir in the rest of the ingredients and cook for 2 to 3 minutes. Serve your tagine right away and enjoy.

Dates and Veggies Stew

Serves: 4 to 6

Ingredients:

- 1 ½ cup of butternut squash, diced
- 1 ½ cup of sweet potatoes, diced
- 1 ½ cup of chickpeas
- 1 cup of green beans
- 1 cup of dates, pitted
- 1 cup of tomatoes, puréed
- 2 tablespoons of honey
- ½ teaspoon of turmeric
- ½ teaspoon of cumin
- ¼ teaspoon of cinnamon
- Black pepper, to taste
- Salt, to taste

Directions:

1. Stir the dates with some boiling water in a small saucepan then cook until they soften.
2. Transfer the soft dates to a tagine with the rest of the ingredients then put on the lid and cook for 40 minutes on low heat.
3. Serve your stew warm and enjoy.

Marrakesh Shakshouka Tagine

Serves: 4

Ingredients:

- 4 eggs
- 450 g of tomatoes, diced
- 1 green bell pepper, roasted and diced
- ¼ cup of water
- 3 tablespoons of vegetable oil
- ½ teaspoon of cumin
- ½ teaspoon of paprika
- ¼ teaspoon of turmeric
- Black pepper, to taste
- Salt, to taste

Directions:

1. Heat the oil in a tagine then cook the tomatoes for 4 minutes.
2. Add the rest of the ingredients, except for the eggs, and stir them to combine the flavors.
3. Put on the lid and let cook for 15 minutes.
4. Use the back of the spatula to create 4 spaces for the eggs in

the tomato sauce then crack an egg in each one.

5. Put on the lid and cook for 10 minutes over low heat or until the eggs are done.

6. Serve your shakshouka tagine warm and enjoy.

Winter Veggies Tagine

Serves: 4 to 6

Ingredients:

- 1 large potato, cut into chunks
- 1 yellow bell pepper, cut into chunks
- 1 red bell pepper, cut into chunks
- 1 eggplant, diced
- 1 zucchini, diced
- 1 yellow onion, thinly sliced
- 2 cups of tomatoes, finely chopped
- 2 cups of water
- 1 cup of chickpeas, canned
- 1 bunch of coriander, finely chopped
- 2 tablespoons of olive oil
- 1 teaspoon of turmeric
- 1 teaspoon of ground ginger
- 1 cinnamon stick
- Black pepper, to taste
- Salt, to taste

Directions:

1. Heat the oil in a tagine and fry the onion for 3 minutes.
2. Add the rest of the ingredients then bring to a boil.
3. Lower the heat and simmer for 25 minutes with the lid on.
4. Serve your tagine with couscous and enjoy.

Chickpea Tagine with White Rice

Serves: 4 to 6

Ingredients:

- 700 g of chickpeas, soaked
- 4 cups of water
- 2 cups of tomatoes, diced
- 1 cup of pumpkin, diced
- 4 tablespoons of coriander, finely chopped
- 3 tablespoons of vegetable oil
- 1 ½ teaspoon of turmeric
- 1 teaspoon of cumin
- 1 teaspoon of ginger
- 1 teaspoon of paprika
- Black pepper, to taste
- Salt, to taste

Directions:

1. Heat the oil in a tagine then cook the tomatoes for 5 minutes until it starts breaking.
2. Stir in the rest of the ingredients then season with salt and pepper.
3. Put on the lid and cook for 40 minutes over low heat.
4. Serve it warm with rice or couscous and enjoy.

Sweet Veggies Tagine

Serves: 4 to 6

Ingredients:

- ◆ 400 g of sweet potatoes, peeled and diced
- ◆ 400 g of zucchini, halved and sliced
- ◆ 1 yellow onion, peeled and chopped
- ◆ 2 cups of veggies broth or water
- ◆ 1 cup of chickpeas, soaked and drained
- ◆ 1 yellow onion, finely chopped
- ◆ 2 tablespoons of oil
- ◆ 2 teaspoons of cumin
- ◆ 1 teaspoon of cinnamon
- ◆ 1 teaspoon of turmeric
- ◆ 1 teaspoon of coriander, ground
- ◆ 1 clove of garlic, minced
- ◆ Black pepper, to taste
- ◆ Salt, to taste

Directions:

1. Combine all the ingredients in a tagine then season with salt and pepper.
2. Put on the lid and let cook for 25 minutes over low heat.
3. Serve your tagine warm with couscous and enjoy.

Saucy Courgette Tagine

Serves: 4 to 6

Ingredients:

- 500 g of small courgettes
- 400 g of white beans
- 2 large tomatoes, finely chopped
- 1 yellow onion, finely chopped
- 1 preserved lemon, sliced
- 1 bunch of coriander, finely chopped
- 4 tablespoons of vegetable oil
- 1 teaspoon of turmeric
- 1 teaspoon of paprika
- 1 teaspoon of cumin
- Black pepper, to taste
- Salt, to taste

Directions:

1. Bring a pot of water to a boil then cook the white beans until they become dent.
2. Heat the oil in a tagine and fry the onion for 3 minutes.

154

3. Drain the white beans and add it to the tagine then add the spices with water and courgettes.
4. Put on the lid and cook for 25 minutes.
5. Pour the chopped tomatoes all over them then put on the lid and cook for 15 minutes over low heat.
6. Serve your courgette tagine warm and enjoy.

Potato and Green Olive Tagine

Serves: 4 to 6

Ingredients:

- 1 ½ kg of potatoes, peeled and diced
- 1 small carrot, diced
- 1 cup of green olives
- 1 onion, chopped
- ½ cup of raisins
- 3 cloves garlic, chopped
- 1 dried red chilli, thinly sliced
- 3 tablespoons of olive oil
- 1 preserved lemon, chopped
- 1 tablespoon cumin seeds, toasted
- ½ teaspoon of ground turmeric
- ½ cup of coriander leaves, chopped
- Black pepper, to taste
- Salt, to taste

Directions:

1. Put the all ingredients except the coriander into a tagine. Mix well then add enough water to just cover.
2. Bring to the boil and put the lid on. Cook for 1 hour over low heat until the potatoes are tender and the mixture is thick.
3. Taste and adjust the seasoning if necessary. Sprinkle with coriander.
4. Serve your tagine warm and enjoy.

Bonus Recipes

This recipe book is strictly about Moroccan Tagines, but what is a Moroccan Tagine without Moroccan bread and preserved lemons? That is why you will not go empty-handed; here are the original recipes of preserved lemons and bread to complete the taste.

Moroccan Bread

Serves: 6

A Moroccan Tagine with Moroccan bread is to die for! It is so easy to make and will take only 15 minutes; it also tastes great with jam, butter, and mint tea.

Ingredients:

- 3 cups unbleached flour
- 1 ½ cups barley flour
- Warm water
- 1 teaspoon dry yeast
- 2 ½ teaspoon salt
- 2 tablespoons olive oil (optional)

Directions:

1. In a big bowl, combine all the ingredients and mix them well with your hands, while adding warm water gradually until you form a slightly stiff dough. Then, allow it to rest so it doubles in size.
2. Sprinkle barley flour on top of your board then divide the dough into 2 and shape into 2 loaves.

3. Allow the 2 loaves to rest until their size starts getting bigger, then place them on a baking sheet.
4. Preheat the oven on 400° F then lower it to 300° F and bake one loaf at a time by placing in it in the middle and allowing it to cook until it becomes dark golden.

Preserved Lemons

Preserved lemon is the remarkable combination of the salty and acidic flavor, which makes it hard to resist; adding it to your recipes will give a new exotic and amazing taste.

Ingredients:

- ♦ 10 lemons
- ♦ 1 cup salt
- ♦ 2 tablespoons olive oil
- ♦ Boiling water
- ♦ 1 canning jar

Directions:

1. Wash the lemons with some boiling hot water then set them aside to dry.
2. Cut each lemon in 4 pieces, but keep it attached at the bottom then fill it with salt.
3. Press the lemons in a canning jar that will keep them pressed tightly.
4. Pour the olive oil on top, secure the lid, and allow your lemon to become preserved.

5. Do not add any water, because the salt will force the lemon to release its juice.
6. Keep them secured in that jar until they become soft and acquire a buttery texture.
7. When you want to use your preserved lemons, do not rinse them. Use them as they are, but do not use salt in your food.

Moroccan Spice Blend

Ingredients:

- 1 teaspoon ginger, ground
- ½ teaspoon cinnamon, ground
- 1 teaspoon cumin
- ¼ teaspoon cloves, ground
- ½ teaspoon coriander seeds, ground
- 1 teaspoon salt
- ½ teaspoon allspice, ground
- ¾ teaspoon black pepper
- ½ teaspoon cayenne pepper

Directions:

Mix all ingredients.

Conclusion

Thank you again for purchasing this book!

If you like Moroccan food or just like to cook different cuisines, I hope you try to cook these tagine recipes and enjoy them.

Moroccans are famous for their incredible tagines, I could not help introducing you to some of these amazing recipes, which are 100% original.

So, whether or not you have visited Morocco, these recipes will make you feel like you are there, and I am sure you will fall in love with them like everyone does.

Made in United States
Troutdale, OR
12/12/2024

26222844R00101